CW00642521

The New Carthaginians

PROLOGUE

Sometimes to understand this world one must turn away from it.
In describing Basquiat's Icarus, Angela Stercken tells us:

As his already quoted understanding of facts indicates, questions of pictorial references
and transmission covering various media soon take centre stage in his work.

And in this reality the trap is to believe in just the facts. How does
that help us? I am at war with their quantization. The truth omits

the unattended moment. I am here to look at the unattended moment.
A painting is a living space of vivid dimension, enclosed, that lets us enter it

and pierces through the volume of our thoughts. It knows there are other
worlds superimposed on our own, as if we were reading off a diagram.

The Ugandan summer of '76 sits in the center. Again, I apologize in advance
for not telling you everything. This only camouflages my discomfort in speaking

to an audience. Black-winged Icarus, the first container, will be our mythology.
Basquiat, the second container, will be my imagination, the new Hi-Tek the new

Bitek. Something in his rapid pace already seems like flight. Therefore, he is valuable
to me. The canvas is our set as seen through the eyes of a bird or the eye of God

(in this world God is not just a being but a state of active consciousness) or the
eye of a poet with a story to tell. But we will need the future too. With respect to

XXXX some names have been changed. Remember, not only the living die. Futures die. So can a past. So can a people – or, worse still, escape into action.

With that paradox as our landscape, we must risk delight. So, with respect to the dead, these events have been told exactly as they occurred.

NICK MAKOHA

The New Carthaginians

PENGUIN BOOKS

PENGUIN BOOKS

UK | USA | Canada | Ireland | Australia
India | New Zealand | South Africa

Penguin Books is part of the Penguin Random House group of companies
whose addresses can be found at global.penguinrandomhouse.com

Penguin Random House UK,
One Embassy Gardens, 8 Viaduct Gardens, London s w 11 7b w

penguin.co.uk

Penguin
Random House
UK

First published 2025
001

Copyright © Nick Makoha, 2025

The moral right of the author has been asserted

Penguin Random House values and supports copyright.
Copyright fuels creativity, encourages diverse voices, promotes freedom
of expression and supports a vibrant culture. Thank you for purchasing
an authorized edition of this book and for respecting intellectual property
laws by not reproducing, scanning or distributing any part of it by any
means without permission. You are supporting authors and enabling
Penguin Random House to continue to publish books for everyone.
No part of this book may be used or reproduced in any manner for the
purpose of training artificial intelligence technologies or systems. In accordance
with Article 4(3) of the DSM Directive 2019/790, Penguin Random House
expressly reserves this work from the text and data mining exception

Set in 9.75/13.5pt Warnock Pro
Typeset by Jouve (UK), Milton Keynes
Printed and bound in Great Britain by Clays Ltd, Elcograf S.p.A.

The authorized representative in the EEA is Penguin Random House Ireland,
Morrison Chambers, 32 Nassau Street, Dublin D02 YH68

A CIP catalogue record for this book is available from the British Library

ISBN: 978-1-802-06706-4

Penguin Random House is committed to a sustainable future
for our business, our readers and our planet. This book is made from
Forest Stewardship Council® certified paper.

TABLE OF CONTENTS

THE DEEP SPACE QUARTET

I.

II.

NOTES

The Deep Space Quartet

I.

Bring your camera.
I am downstairs. Bring cash.
The meter's running.

flight | ˈflʌɪt

1 [flight] *(There are things that can never be the same, like the history of space.)* 2 A M. This is the actual

moment when Basquiat and I first meet. In the light of that moment, he begins to talk about doing

something other than art: writing perhaps. I take his coffee and cup it in one hand as he draws a pair

of wings on the back of a napkin. Why wings? I ask. *Because this body is an imperfect container.*

2 [flight] *(Time is what stops everything from happening at once.)* I remember Icarus, Iverson's 48-point game,

the taste of sorrel on a beach, but I have forgotten the fear of flying. I wake from a deep sleep,

conscious I am an animal. A bird on fire looking for an edge. For the third time in my life, I am

scissoring through darkness. The night is thick with everything coming. Swift is the night. Slow is the dark.

3 [flight] *(Fleeing.)* Think of it like this: Amelia, the flight attendant, will want to know if everyone is O K.

My face framed in the mirror of an Airbus bathroom lacks courage. A gun in a paper bag. All things

fear you and tremble in your presence. As my life has taught me, we must suffer. Without this world,

I will take myself and unhinge myself from this body. (Keep in mind that this section is translated.)

4 [flight] *(Between floors or levels.)* I didn't get to choose the location, 0.0436° N, 32.4418° E in its darkness

and hunger. Neither did I choose the ceiling of stars that made me a foreigner that evening. In the same

way that the air becomes something else the moment we lean into it. Waiting to bear
   us up as we glide
upon it. Then I too am a new thing born of another language. I am both familiar and
   unfamiliar.

5 ^{flight} *(A selection of small portions.)* This photo was taken towards the end of the shoot.
   It is a Love Movement.
If you add captions under the sound of the rain pounding you can hear my father ask
   the cameraman,
Will the light displace us? Stevie Wonder is playing. I am off-camera and at three years
   old I already
know they are going to split up. That Uganda skyline looks completely different now.

6 ^{flight} *(A far-fetched idea.)* Who understands the world? The year is 1976. It will be a
   long summer.
Air France Flight 139 will depart from Tel Aviv. So far, no sign of blood. The future,
   what does it know?
We are in the last stages of waiting. A German will ask for the freedom of forty
   Palestinians detained in Israel.
They are moving to a changed destination, a foreign city that houses the room in which
   I was born.

7 ^{flight}*(The tail.)* Do you know this one? I call it Icarus's theme tune.

He flies away like a dream, and they cannot find him;
Even like a vision of the night, he is chased away.
Job 20:8

'76

I.

If this is what we know, then their year is 1976 and the air is thick
with everything coming. If this is not a war, then there will be
no need for an enemy. If there is a hero, then there will be death.
If history, being what it is, demands a hero, we could use the
DeLorean to jump back into time. If only it were that simple.
Then this text would be the experiment in which we are studying
time. It passes more slowly the more you are moving. I used to be
a scientist. Consider, for example, how light emitted from an existing
source admits a lower frequency. I am moving. When you change
your cause, you rotate the direction of time. This is how time

II.

behaves when it is rotated – it becomes relative. We will begin
with a plane because you might have heard one pass your window.
What is flying but a way to climb the air? We are at 30,000 feet
on Flight 139. What do you know of the Revolutionary Cell?
What do you know of Athens airport? What do you know about
Operation Thunderbolt? You may or may not have heard of Yoni
and what happened in 1976. In the movie, Yoni is the hero. Known
terrorists are the enemies led by Bose. We are seven days away
from the 4th of July but this is not an American story. We are
heading to a foreign town on an airport runway on the same day

III.

The Real Thing tops the charts with 'You To Me Are Everything'.
The song will spend three weeks at No. 1. You might be
asking, *What does that band have to do with the terrorist operation?*
It is in the first line: *I would take the stars out of the sky for you.*
I want to tell you about the sky. I want to tell you about the
sounds of leaving. I may talk about Basquiat and what he knew
of Icarus. I don't know where to begin so I may jump around
in search of a source code, in search of a known life, in search of
fire and something to displace us. There will be foreign dying.
But before we begin with these segments here is a commercial break.

Codex© of Birds

In the first part of the night, I saw the coastal villages, men arguing
about the price of oil and swifts darting into shadows. Their repeated
outlines cast them into flight. When I was the night, when I was the seeker
in the void, I took shape. The sun and day were no longer witnesses.
It was the only way I knew to catch the world's attention. In a universe
filled with light, I belonged to things that burn. That is my alibi. Trees rose
over my eyelashes. The sky was filled with night. There was a time when
I thought that to release myself from my self and its boiling rage I had to
become the sort of animal that swallowed expensive wine from mason jars.

        In that doubling, I began to master the speech of birds
in the same way that a pilot draws darkness down. Imagine the body
just passing through. Imagine a kiss that binds one animal to another.
Delicious because it was hers. I was no easy prey, like an engine
questioning its parts. Be flock, be mouth, be the shadow. The questions
you ask as you coil in a cabin – What does living do to a country
that is no longer here as you push away from the earth? How can you
reverse the direction of the heart? Once, on a plane, when I was younger,
as the sky unfastened from its edge, I saw the sea as a boundary and an ending,
as the hostess passed words from one mouth to another. Each flight
a reincarnation. And now I am the sky.

Basquiat asks the Poet about Death

At a rooftop party, the night is the night, and we are watching death.
Or should I say Bruce Willis is walking barefoot in a skyscraper?
I wish I had taken a picture. The host, some newscaster you would
recognise from TV, has hired a firm to project the film onto the hotel
wall across the street. My date has just returned from the bathroom.
I am her plus one. Pointing to the open bar, I can feel the sun's heat
reflecting off the building. She has me speaking in my fourth language
but my thoughts have us undressed in my first. By the pool, a waiter asks
Are you ready to order? You recommend the Pad Thai with chicken
for two and if they are out of that you say we'll go for the snapper with
a snake-bean salad. DJ Shadow is connecting speakers to his decks when
his left elbow knocks the Blood Orange Champagne Mule to the concrete.
Even falling has its grace. Bruce Willis is at the top of the Nakatomi building.
Terrorists intend to blow it up. He is ready to face a paradox. A building burning
is a way of saying *you're not welcome here.* The waiter returns with our cutlery.
I can see my country in the steel with only weeks to go before it's bankrupt.
As if I needed the reminder that I can be in two places at once.

Pegasus[1]

A friend of mine who was not yet ready to visit his friend in another life insists that the West[2]

had a good working relationship with the regime.[3] His wife had worked for some politician.

Or was it, his wife dated some politician? And now the politician wouldn't return her calls.[4]

Skin like midnight, waist like a moving river, eyes like coloured glass. They had met over drinks

just before the coup in January of that year at a conference upstate.[5] Now they had him in custody[6] –

the politician – on suspicion of *normalising proceedings*. Whatever that means. This is his mug shot.

Staged, of course. Something was missing. With no lawyer present, the police made sure they showed

him some African hospitality.[7] They loosened their ties and tuxedos but not their shoes and fed him *posho*

with *nyama choma*. They even washed his hands with the good water.[8] You can't have hospitality

without a cold beer. I have tried. They drank to his future. They drank to fast love because he mentioned

---

1 *Now is The Time*
2 (The first illusion.)
3 At their command, nothing escaped. Time refuted its dimension and became a distance between points.
4 She didn't know that selfish ambition imitates a narcotic dream.
5 She opened up as one would to the god-like entities in Kubrick's *Space Odyssey*,
6 weightless and transformed into some sort of reverse superman.
7 Outside that window the sky continued to grow.
8 Much later they would become heavier entities in the world.

the wife's name. They drank till he showed the other side of himself. On this side of
  paradise, nothing
is offered without reward.[1] They filled their blood with mercury. Or was it they filled
  their blood

with war? *There must be some kind of mistake,* the politician insisted. His face was the
  moon.[2]
And to think just a few weeks ago he had got his golf handicap down to ten. This is a
  man
Who, normally, everyone believed: a man with a philosophy.[3] A man who spoke like
  he had a secret,

who once was shown a diagram, given to him by his secretary (all five foot seven and
  one hundred
and ninety one pounds of her). Confidential blueprints were a currency with which to
  negotiate.[4]
But he didn't play that game. This is a photograph of the politician in an upstairs room
  next to a vase

filled with dahlias. They're with a reporter now who is trying to fill in the blanks.
  Satellite photos
of a field and fighter planes that plunge like arrows lead us to an unarmed Swiss bank
  account.
Code name Pegasus.[5] Perhaps Hegel was right when he said – *The finite world is a reflection
  of the mind.*[6]

---

1 A plane drifted downwards – birds came into sight – the no-smoking sign came on.
2 Hijackers argued about money as blood rushed through their ears.
3 Now a low burning flame.
4 Time must never be thought of as pre-existing.
5 This must be a mistake?
6 Even the darkness hides its face as the sound of the storm moves away.

Option

What are airports really? Late June and you are not
where you are supposed to be. The old airport building

is rough to the touch. Day two. Don't say it. I know
I should be ordering room service from the Ritz Carlton.

I'm in the mood for steaks with fries and some frozen yogurt.
The direct flight was an extra 300 drachma, despite the fact

my wife and I are in the old departure lounge with our eyes
closed while hostages search for our passports. The good news

is I will be missing my brother-in-law's wedding. That prick
takes us all to dinner, kids too, and thinks he is doing me

a favour. When I pour expensive wine on his Persian rug,
he smiles and says that things, unlike people, are easily replaced.

Their cars have leather seats – in this heat. He pays for the children
to go to private school. They come home fortnightly and go on

three family holidays minimum and not a grey hair to show for it.
If he was here, I bet he would be discussing stock options with

the hostages and upselling them life insurance dressed in
a tuxedo. Hmm. That reminds me. I need to draw up my will.

1.

I am from the earth and so are the trees. That is my alibi. Sometimes I can feel it the way one country feels the border of another. But since the myth of me is uncategorised, you can call me the Kampala Kid who at one time hated the mountains and the hills and the red dust they shed. What a cruel fate for a son of paradise to be caught in its heat but unable to breathe.

2.

Watch the sky's indifference and the sun's eclectic stare as I puff on my Ventolin inhaler. If you press your ear to my heart, you can hear it whisper – *do not destroy me.* And in that thought the Black astronaut is born with the wish for his body to fly away. Think of another myth with the same root. I am climbing a tall fence when I should have stayed at home. In my back pocket is all the money I have in the world, less my bus fare home. I am at the neighbourhood drive-in looking for a blue Volkswagen Beetle. My date is in a Volkswagen Beetle looking for me. As she opens the passenger door to an empty seat her eyes say, *take it.* Or, a more accurate translation – *I pick you for my people.*

3.

Let me start again. When the journalist asks the warlord –
is this peace just the meat between two wars? Watch his
pupils fly to the back of his head. One of the side-
effects of salbutamol is time curving into itself. The first
time it happened was by the Nile. When I talk of river
it is always the Nile, even when I am in another city
looking at a puddle reflecting me back. I would like to
suggest that when MJ dunks from the free-throw line
he is doing what Léon Foucault calls flattening time.

4.

Back at the Nile my words become creatures resonating
in space. I wonder if da Vinci experienced this when he
drew the flying machine. Freehand.

Icarus talks to the poet on
Rodeo Drive about leaving

We arrive back late at night.
Basquiat is bent in prayer.
A canvas hung on the wall.

The late L.A. sunset has found
my face. He is whispering
something about how his paintbrush

is the tip of a spear or the tip
of the world at dusk. A wingbeat,
the caves, the wind: in fact all falling

is an act of flight. DaVinci knew that.
Because winged men falling through
a membrane of sky was part of Milton's

dream. Ovid was an eyewitness.
He knew exile was a way of saying,
my country is beautiful, or *the distance*

kills me. Above the outskirts of a city,
who wants to become a missing
thing? To leave this place you must take

something and break it. In the time of myth,
I was dead. When I was a boy, I was dead.
When I was a parable, and a painting,

I was dead. Only Basquiat saw me at the edge
of the world, and did not turn away when
the sky was a window as it has always been.

A True Account[1]

JFK   LAX to JFK. A warrior wind is seeking what we have lost but the pilot has
         the
      wings of the redeye under his command. As the night flickers on – The world

      below widens – bat-like[2] – I wonder what the night sees in me – A thing that
         flies
      from earth to pour its pain into an island smaller than this one – You

      don't always get the story you want even when the runway changes – Once,
      in a type of beginning, after The Roots concert but before check-in – I packed

      my bag the way I pack my heart – There it lay on the bed – towel around
      my waist – At check-in, the stewardess with perfect posture handed me back

      my passport as if it were weightless[3] – Actually, more than once I have packed
      my heart in a bag hoping that it could inhabit a body/memory/island bigger

      than this one – If I stay still for too long the body hardens the way that

----

1 *of a Hijacking at Entebbe Airport*
2 It begins with a SLOGAN like THE CITY NEVER SLEEPS and a descending prayer call
whispering in the wind and an idea that works – entrusted to the bodyguard at the temple – as a
people attempt to become a modern imperial state. Now, whether they will succeed will depend
on how they enter the next scene. Ammunition prices have risen dramatically. In an upswept
house a woman enters from the street outside with her first-born cradled in her arms. Her streets
like mine are filled with security – men with old rifles.
3 Does that make us kin? She uncovers her face and shuts the rest of the world out. This is what I
have learnt: the man who sleeps in her bed will be dead in week. Unlike Ulysses, he will not come
home from the war. When the space his heart takes becomes a leaking red dot, she will swear
she saw his face in the clouds. Women will think she is talking to the sun (whose power it is to
make the gods afraid) with its red centre. For a while they will entertain it when she writes in the
sand – *I have watched over you.*

black cake does when you don't follow the recipe[1] – Dear friends, although I
    pick

at my lunch it does not alter the natural order of things – This flight bears
the sweetness of wings[2] but it is not a cure for exile – If I were to say how
    much

further? – it would make no difference – As we descend toward the
    shoreline,
read my eyes like a clock – surely the sky in its appetite is open to us?

---

1 But this is not the shield of Achilles or the Star of David. When beetles see its glow, they run backward into the dark. What is the purpose of an empty field? Mr Cain, my science teacher, would look me in the face as if the boats were coming in and say – *A field is a numerical property of an extended part of the universe.* The smart aleck in me would ask – Do you know how to get there from here? My family picked cotton in a field. Here – a dark sky. There is an airfield. He – who she calls her shield – has now a battered body.

2 Dear circus, dear night of the blooming flower, dear dark sky, and dear country to which I have not returned, dear thought in which the vinegar of my consciousness swims – take me back to the cockpit and the pilot with a gun pointed to his head. Why does he not break loose when he and his crew are offered freedom? Instead, in the weight of that dimension, he says words that like twilight are worth repeating – What I am is not important. And in that delicate frequency with lowered guns, they give him back his life.

AMS

We are falling to earth. The headrest
TV display is a jukebox. Night pins
itself to the plane. My earphones
drown an audience of men who have
turned my homeland into a theatre.
Their mouths are full of salt and lime,
swimming through my body weight
in tequila. A low-pressure system
at the level of my abdomen watches
them from my cabin window. Ryan
Gosling is at the keys. My hands want
to be at their throats. They are gods
in a City of Stars. No wait, I am a city
watching three men play God. No, I am
God watching three men play with my city.

II.

Flight is the tendency to move
toward or away from an object.
As in Basquiat's Icarus, for instance.
Notice how everything turns away.

Primer

This is a living memory. Sometimes I enter a day blade first. Like abracadabra.
Disappear the moonlight, let the sun burn the way a field burns itself clean.
I'm no fortune teller but here is my diagnosis. We are in the middle of a dry month

and as you know a dry heat has a few side-effects. The Passing – A dry cough – Are
you finding it hard to sleep – What about the night sweats – Some of the ones you
    love
will not make it to the second act. No wonder you are afraid. No wonder you keep

trying to pierce throughout the veil of time. Does every box have to be ticked
for you to believe that I am the protagonist? Fun fact – my people are not the belly
of a fruit. Fun fact – Black Death is not a toy to play with. We are not auditioning

to be the Holy Ghost. On that note, *Goodfellas* is not just about Italians, just as Black
Panther is really about something you can't have. Isn't it funny that you hold all
the cards? – Direct democracy, the earth as far as the mountain ranges, even the
    banks

still hold your names. But you still hold a weak hand because you don't believe.
When you drink from our power does it help you perform the dance of safety?
To imitate the night the way a cave mimics the night once you enter it.

Riddle Me This, Batman

The other night as my room faded to silence and my skin cooled, I dreamt that my father was the River Nile and I walked across him toward the trees in the distant panorama. How do I know it was my father? Because of what the river wanted from me. Later my thoughts returned to me as I drank a glass of water. That too wanted something from me. So, I returned to the dream and my father the river and asked (I did that a lot throughout my childhood, mostly in the belly of a

plane)[1] – Was Joseph, the interpreter of dreams, an alien? Freud points out that *it is in fact never possible to be sure that a dream has been completely interpreted.* Cut to a January where sixty Karimojong warriors are in a conflict over pasture and scarce sources of water. Among the dead[2] are twenty women and

---

1 FALLEN ANGEL
Or maybe being the Batman is a way of stepping out of his life. The way when an Uber driver waving a placard for Mr McCola (close enough) calls your name. You can be someone new when he says – *So what do you do?* You can change the tide. Isn't that a tide's purpose: to cover, discover and recover? After eight hours in standard class, you are sitting in the back seat watching a new city come towards you. The DJ on the radio is asking you to get ready for the weekend. In this failing world you go to Plan B. Take the next left – (I would like to fly out of my head the way Joyce Bryant used to sing out of her head after a doctor sprayed her throat with cocaine.) – Who's prepared to pay the price for a trip to paradise? – Love for Sale. I'm fed up with hiding behind my eyes. Do you ever notice the sea turning to rain? I pull up the collars of my trench coat the same way the Batman uses his heavy black cloak to escape gravity. Is that how one enters paradise?

2 BIRD OF PARADISE
I was never dead. This is not a small dark-faced bird or the quiet asking the darkness, *who is that Black man with wings?* This is a Black man returning to his dream. A dream carved into the month of June, or the gates of June as if I were a wax figure. Who, when the moment was ripe, was easily made. But I am not a manmade thing. I came back because I was ready to connect history to art the way moonlight connects the sky to the sea. Or maybe I was just hedging my

twelve children. The problem is you are not interested in what I know or what I don't know, only in what survives. I wish that were a dream. They burn the bodies. A man on fire is not the same as

a man under fire. Do the warriors in 1967 differ from what happened in 1976? Here is where one thought becomes two. I often wonder what the one word was that The Jackal said to Dr Wadi'a Haddad that had him removed from the Entebbe hijacking. Considering that The Jackal was the sort of man who would glide to the centre of a room with a gin and tonic in hand. I wonder if the same word would make my father return.

---

bets. As a rule, many are cautious of life. What I mean is I have been cautious with life and I command you not to fear the way life moves through space. Why fear the hawk when it is the wind that carries him? Why fear the photograph when it is the camera that sees you? And even that is not the truest eye. Especially when you are badly drawn. In order to survive ourselves, my father laid down lines of feathers so that they imitated real bird's wings. That part is true. So, flight was fitted on the boy's shoulders like the sun folding into the day's horizon. That is also true. Becoming a man who passes himself off as bird? Watch the sky become night, watch the night become silk. By dawn it falls away through empty air. To our right an airport hides its self-interest. Awaiting the night's return.

Icarus at the Fun Gallery in the East Village of New York

Fuck it, let's start with Canto 27:
Now upward rose the flame, and still'd its light.

Two birds perched on a jeep in the West Bank
catch the air and migrate to the shores of Entebbe.

Have you ever decided anything in the air?
Neither intelligence nor intimidation are sufficient.

I bet da Vinci when writing *The Codex of Birds*
would gather the most curious member of the audience

and ask of them – *take my hand . . .angle my arm just so
and flex the wing.* I know they thought this was about birds.

If you calculate your power the small can stand up to the large.
Here's an angle: my father used to say he would catch me

looking into the sky searching for its bounds to calm
my tightened lungs after the asthma attack. It was here

I discovered the wind and the falling body and the urge
to run across the sky. Imagine a pilot ejecting from a plane -

Stay with me now. At that moment of release, his back wishes
he was a feathered thing. That is what I almost became.

The Long Duration of a Split Second

Because all language lacks fluency in this pretence the sky itself was wilderness.
A camera with its crooked frame was the first eye searching for answers. In this
margin of the day, a helicopter unsure of how to get out of the world glided

down through cloud cover and became a second infrared eye. Its purpose,
to separate people from trees and hills, still warm with the day's heat, from
shadows. Men dressed for war used torches like fireflies to follow

the echoes. Inside a whisper – revenge. Inside revenge – a language. Inside
the language – an algorithm of how to turn a collage of startling images
into a village of some importance. A car horn shrieked like an unfed child

to introduce the theory of infinite endings. Within that horn an eruption
and within that eruption another. Then fourteen seconds of darkness –
before the camera reproduced men in the motion of battle. He who

conforms to loss of land must be the right enemy. It is easier to divide
the world this way. A disobedient tribe explain their extinction in the desert.
To begin the story again, what was once a village on a rock they will call Jerusalem.

But who discovered you? Outside the thermal frame, a woman's voice cries out.
Four gunshots, made visible by a cloud of hot air, to invent a new kind of time.
Paradise and violence are the same road: one cannot exist without the other, both

gladly accept loss. A bullet has found its currency spiralling up toward a moving
vehicle whose engine has died. Getting away is what a road is for. A car door
opened to the wilderness and so this hill became a portrait of death. A fatal bullet
turned the driver into the shape of someone else. The flowers blame themselves.

Self Portrait[1] of[2]

If I'm going to sing like someone else,
then I don't need to sing at all. – E. Faga

---

1 *1981* That midsummer and the D'Angelo concert is sold out at Brixton. Fuck! I can't tell you what he whispered to security but here's a picture of Icarus and me backstage with two press cards pinned to our chests. And to think four hours ago I was clocking off work. They have only just let in the crowd. You can hear the hum through the tannoy. The thing about Icarus is he has a microchip for a mouth. You say it he

will name it. You name it he will play it. Once after his dad had died I caught him beating his chest after a month of fasting and prayer. They were more like songs really – the way the words fell away from his bones. Anyway, he is calling Keyon Harrold, the trumpet player from The Vanguard, 'Kenya'. Asking him things like *How do you create an open field in the band* and if he believes in the equation of the Freedom Principle

even in light of *the Palestine situation.* D'Angelo has popped two cassettes into a deck. Icarus calls him Smoke. My bladder is about to cut loose. When I return, they are huddled around the tape deck like tribesmen eating jerk chicken, listening to a jamming session from the morning's rehearsal in silence. Smoke must have taken the picture because he is the only one not in it. Icarus is in the centre with his wings fanning and closing.

[2] the poet as Cassius Clay 1982

To forgive someone requires two incidents in your life. The most obvious is the incident that like fire must be redeemed by fire. Here's the match. A young journalist is speaking to camera – but her eyes struggle to find the centre. She is talking about my country the way a wino pees Pepsi into a can. This is being broadcast round the world. Except for the countries she is in. Hmm! She's using her diaphragm to say things outside the range of her common experience. We are what you talk about before you cut to the news desk for an update on the Olympics. The only part you will remember is that the Queen's daughter

has qualified for the British riding team. And not that the body on the ground belonged to another body. And that he fought to stay alive the way the journalist fights with her mic or fights to beat the falling darkness or fights away a pair of mosquitoes that hover between her breast and right eye – hover between her lip and right breast. The cameraman has the engine running and is using the back of the pickup as a tripod while he rolls himself a smoke. Watch his lens searching for the sweetness of death. If only the dead could awaken. The lighter belongs to the body on the ground, so do the smokes, and

so does the country in which we watch him. The mosquitoes know this – that is why they are unhinged – and now so do you. The second point of forgiveness sits in the future like the woman I will one day love and the country in which I will one day live. Forgive me. My heart is a vicious wolf that moves like the cloud of God searching for the true shape of history searching for the weight of a love lost. My mother was a river, my father was a boat – both separated by a sack of light

Julius Caesar

I believe that James McAvoy is a type of Caesar. But he never stays
in character long enough to make it hold. Now when pirates had
Caesar caught in a trap off the coast of Rhodes, he demanded that
they ask for more than double the ransom. When Caesar says,
do this, it is performed. These fishermen, his kidnappers (is 'kidnapped'
too strong?), accept his request as he recited poetry to them on a throne
of flour. Two months after paying the ransom, with the aid of a private

army, he squeezed the yolk out of these men. We're doomed. I know
we can't all be Moses but have you noticed that superstars always want to
play our parts. There's this dialogue where Nicholas Garrigan, played
by McAvoy, is rebuked by Idi Amin – *You promised to me you would help me
build a new Uganda.* McAvoy doesn't answer. Don't you know that that's
how they take us? It is Bura's Desperado Sacrifice. *Forcing the Black king
to h8 doesn't seem to accomplish much, but it makes all of the difference*

in just two moves. (1. Qh8+ 2. Rxa1 3. Bxe7.) Crossing a runway is not
like crossing the street, especially when your Black king is a counterfeit
played by Forest Whitaker and his lazy eye. Planes have been hiding in
the air. This duty-free gin is a useless placebo. But rumour has it Miss
America Tawny Godin from Yonkers has a smile you want all to yourself.
The thing about my country is that there is always somebody ready to say
– *You're mine.* Maybe I should have led with that. Anyway, it's your move.

Warrior

When in doubt surrender. There goes the future
taking a lead role, hiding planes in the air. An hour
from now a soft-voiced wind in its vanilla musk
will raise a colony of bats by their wings. An hour
from then they will be over the Rift Valley and as
the day turns, soldiers from another war (unmarried boys)
will hide in the heavy black cloak wondering – is this
how it really ends? How in the name of spirit and fire
are the clouds here cloudless? Isn't that a pair of dice?
Last night men who had not yet tired of being brave
broke into the old airport leaving nothing but mirrors.
This was not a performance despite the dress rehearsal.
No warrior asks to be the smoke without the fire. As the eye
slow turns notice how time draws a veil over the future.

Basquiat asks the Poet to Paint him the Truth

They just cast Charles Bronson because he's going down
well in Europe. I knew we weren't going to get straight
answers. The war reporters were selling democracy and asking
for the copyright to a Ugandan stage set in which we had minor

parts (third villager, English-speaking native, and if they can make
it to the third act, soon-to-be refugee). Then the reporters returned
to their desks and the IDF agents returned the hostages to their lives
and they left my country where it was and the plane on the tarmac.

Basquiat's wings had turned jet black at that time. And I when I told
the director this country was ours to begin with, I could smell alcohol
on his breath. My shoulder blades itched. I hadn't started growing feathers.
I drew diagrams to explain my choices. When he showed me the bulletins -

the Palestine situation, the price of oil, the American Embassy's
concerns about the disruption of international trade by hijackers -
my body wanted to be in my country instead of above it. Like Icarus above
the sea where the sky in all versions of itself is blue even when it wasn't.

The New Carthaginian

Black men of Carthage, Ethiopia,
of Timbuktu and Alexandria gave the
likes of civilization to this world.

Marcus Garvey

We are slaves to the world engine. Nothing eludes it. It has us in synchronous labour. Since birth our dark matter settling into itself. Each one of us let fall, a pyramid removed from its original purpose. Yielding as petals do from a flower's bloom. Some want us dead and will do what is required to fulfil that purpose.

Remember when they smoked our bodies like cigars, remember when they tore us from ourselves like loose clothing, remember when they wore our women like jewels and in the same adornment scattered them as one would dust among the stars. And what of the children? You question me. Maybe I am making this up as one does a dream. Maybe I am a broken king burning in the embers of his own rage. You are right. One of these is true. Would you call a body hanging from a tree an imitation of Christ on the cross? Both were killed for something they did not do.

What is the crime: believing the story or wanting to know the truth? Let us enter through another door. Look, a mirror. Now let us see ourselves as we really are. To stand in the window of oneself and draw yourself into a new shape. Let the storm brew: lean in. You are not a fridge magnet in a duty-free store or the handle of a dull blade. Hold that note. In this place you are no longer the chorus. Let this world be your hammer. In any future, remember: you are a New Carthaginian.[1]

Exit: Hannibal

---

1 *Blackness here is not a term of intimacy or human vagary but of publicness.* – Kevin Quashie

III.

The story of your own birthplace,
a country twice erased, once by fire,
once by forgetfulness, it probably means
you are standing too close.
Li-Young Lee, 'Behind My Eyes'

Riding With Death

Against men who need no solace. In the middle of
July they found the knife that killed you. The kill was
close. Death would not enter of its own accord. It
had to be coaxed like an old king. It did not know
their customs, only what my heart knows as it
searches for a word for *enter*. You know that late
reaction, that is unable to change in water but
readily burns in air – "Why does a man do what he
does?" What is it that the spirits want with him? In
these last eight minutes of your life, you now
trespass on the earth and its furniture. Hold no
grudge. Those shallow breaths betray you and your
clenched wrists. Your dark eyes wish to be owned
again but look what they have become. Death will
not greet you with trumpets and drums. Watch
death and its small entourage!

An Essay on Man

Maybe the measure of life's brief sequence
can be found in the mist that hangs over trees
as their branches twist in the wind. A jealous
fire ploughs through an abandoned warehouse
and pays no attention to the security guard.
His dying eyes growing wide, betraying their duty.
Everything floods through. His ex-wife wonders
how it happened. The policemen at the door
ask for a glass of water. Biting her top lip,
she lets the evening in and offers them broken
rice with fried chicken and coleslaw. As the stars
appear, with their mouths full of food, the clock
will chime. Despite the heat of the day they
eat the meat to the bone. You are right to ask
the question. Why share the favourite meal of
the man she once loved? Let me place before
you one or two things; the eye hungers for what
it can't find as a wave of delivery trucks roars to
a stop. This lady throws a window open, puts on
his old coat and takes a drag from a cigarette she
would never smoke. If it wasn't for the fence you
would see her out on the porch tucking her hair
behind her left ear, holding the smoke that fits
inside her body. What does she need it for?
It is the last wave of the man who lived inside her.

Icarus asks Basquiat to Paint Him

Is it strange to miss yourself? In their ignorance,
they remember my flight: they see me as a fallen
angel with the sea ready to catch me. Disappearing
has become my life. Come closer. Your bloodshot
eyes are filled with prescriptions. Is this who you
have always been? If I am honest, I was afraid
of meeting you. As I walked through the door,
I saw you scribbling a beating heart on the border
of a textbook. Better that than being pinned to a
white-walled gallery imitating death. We can
eat first if you like. The Cajun chicken sandwich
is five stars. Put that away. It's on me. What I'm
about to tell you I need you to commit to memory:
I did not desert this life. I was driven from it like

a god from his people. When I last spoke my mother
tongue I was a child. Then the words left my mouth.
It was then that I became a bird. It is easier to be
a machine than a bird. But when the earth does not
want you, then to the air you go. I wish it would
return, the way the sun does to the noon. After the fall
I remember the highway and my disturbed mind, and
how my bones itched and how the weight of who I was
could not hold the weight of who I was to become.
Make sure they see me as you see me now. Look what
the sky holds. When I was the morning bird and there
was light I did not run. When I was the black astronaut,
against the sky, I did not run. Here come our orders.
What do you want to drink? Could we have two Cognacs?

Documenta 7[1]

After three months in Cairo, I was already
caught in a trap. It would have been easier
to execute a lunar landing in reverse. This is

me listening to a long note getting louder
as I walk towards a field. This is me sipping
coffee quickly to cure my fears. My shoes

look pathetic. Why does coffee in a glass
eclipse coffee in a cup? This is me in the corner
of a bar saying things like: get up out of your body.

Get out of the prison cell. Get out of the furnace
of this world. Even when I decorate the space
with music the nightmares still fly out of my head.[2]

This is me in the back of a taxi with a mountain girl,
who tonight will use my body as a throne. I am too
familiar with this body, I take its concerns for granted.

---

1 I watch a montage of the moon and clouds at the edge of darkness.

Icarus ESSO
2 In short, they would have you believe that nothing actually moves through time.
Even when I was a boy falling out of the sky devoid of a moon. In the used light,
the sky was a red I had never seen. A red usually reserved for war. This sky was
something that death could not kill. Look at the shape it throws and how it asks
me to be the chorus. The wind nudged me off this black earth as ospreys arced
the sky over the hills. Above the souk filled with traders I became a weight
and a measure. In this failing world my brittle wings were a dark cloak. Now that
I am at the cliff's edge watch how they convulse and quiver: watch how I disappear.

Nora

In the mid-'70s I was a nobody with a foreign accent.
The sort of person you only recognise in a hardware store
when you need to know in which aisle you can get

one of these, as you show me the picture of Jane Fonda's
bathroom. I'd be the guy in brown overalls demanding
higher pay, but not demanding higher pay because that's

how the last nobody lost his job. So, I point you to aisle
7 and ask Nora at the register to turn the radio up.
It's not as good as a pay rise, but they are playing Nora's

favourite song. Don't ask me why I notice the smell of her
body among other bodies or why I stay late to help her
with the stock check. She's quite demanding. I don't say

anything, it's better that way. With the change in my pocket,
I take her yawns as a cue to order two coffees. I don't like coffee,
it tastes like tar on my tongue. She adds three sachets of sugar,

slips off her shoes and offers me some gum. It's not until the gum
has lost its flavour that her eyes dilate to let more light in. I feel
like an ancient star waiting for this part of the night to happen.

The History of Black People

This is not the bullet's story or a view of Mars. Call this evidence
or a river. The night before the river functioned as an eye. Time

is a river in which the past is always flowing. But the function
of the eye in this world is to draw whatever is placed in front of it.

Wait there to watch how money changes hands. Who knows what
running water thinks or its afterthoughts? A house waits for a boy

who will not return. His body leaks heat. A stubborn wind demands
to be heard. How else can an evening in its own darkness present a boy's

body at rest? Ghosts are signs of a hurried life. The flesh in search
of its own interior. As this evening drops to earth and midges come to life,

follow the money. I'll guide you there myself, past the khaki police and
the lake's drying lip, past the forest that fed us well, past these wild grasses

and the hawk's descent, past the body of Christ pinned to a wall. Look what
it hides, primitive thatch, hills that grow from continuous silence. The silence

of a turning world, or two stars passing behind clouds. It sits within us.
A prayer without words. It leads you to the Black familiar. Look at its diameter.

In good hands, lovers run into the bushes; in good hands, there is an abundant
harvest from forgotten grain; in good hands, a man's name is as precious as gold;

in good hands, we can't watch the black outline of the sun. You've passed this way
yourself to gain the advantages of war. Joseph Conrad would have us believe

it's to keep the world safe. He'll convince *The Times* these are the margins,
that is the border and this is us aligned in close order. But you be the judge.

Moses and the Egyptians

I am framed by a body that frames my heart.
But no one sees its temperature, its working curve

or how the heat softens. The story goes that when Moses
was handed the tablets he asked his scything tongue

to adopt an identical twin. A double who did not speak.
He did not eat to aid his seeing. Let me set the scene –

Three continents are behind that cloud. His only companions
the wild goats and the bird-folk darting like arrows

into the empty air. His steps cool along the mountain face.
Eager to reach the summit. Each foot gathering

its steadiness like a stallion clearing a fence in a field.
Even when it rained and the fringe of his black cloak dragged

along the earth and the floor was mud, he moved. Upward,
towards the clouds, pressing his heels into the mud

even when the song of the wind pushed him to the edge.
In the charity of this hard moment he did not turn back.

The Poet and Basquiat Plan a Trip to Venice

At check-in, they ask for the American, a makeshift character
trapped in his living shape. Earlier on the platform, I followed
him through the smoke down the steps at Columbus Circle, paint
on his fingernails and passport in hand. We stand with our backs
to the world, watching our reflections, 14ft of wings tucked into
our jackets. Sometimes we are not moving at all. Heavy shadows
cast like dark angels. Occasionally he pulls his headphones off to
play me an instrumental (his version of prayer). A shiver catches
me. It is my last touch of the world before we arrive at Port Authority,
where the sound of the wind follows the sound of the wind as we
follow a lady in high heels to the desk. For luggage, we have two
spray cans, three sticks of gum and a notebook. At 30,000 feet
I feel the hum of the wing knifing through the black night.

He says we should be out there.

Equals pi

1.

The three of us paddle in our kayaks to Pumgume Island. Before the third morning, the future separates into sea and sky. In the fractured extension of broken time, everything depends on how you interpret it, just as a prayer is more than the order of its words. Take that corner of the sky –

notice how the brightness of a gleaming sun retreats from the world? The journey picks us up in Stone Town where all our food and drinks are catered. A lone fisherman beckons us to the far side of the beach. In the brief history of his silence, we set up camp for the night as the fisherman

tends to a fire under the baobab trees. I fall asleep to the flame. What if the spaces we use for testimony are equal to *pi*? Here is a burning bush. Moses was a fugitive who saw the whole of Egypt's harvest destroyed. He stood against a troop of magicians and had to believe that the God

2.

who called to him from the flames of a burning thicket would terraform his reality. In the brief history of this other silence, he was talking to God, in the same way I'm talking to you. What theatre, to catch God mid-sentence. I wonder if he stresses his Ts? I wonder if when Kanye burns

his childhood home to rubble on stage if he is really drawing a line, a parallel to a burnt city which equals *pi*. What if the burning bush was God's cover blown? Or what if the flames were God's primer and the flames' crackle was the soundscape he embodied while he awaits another voice? The kind

of voice you might hear coming out of the drum kit of Max Roach while recording *Money Jungle* in the now. By now I mean, today is equal to *pi*. The pistol of a dead man is equal to *pi*. The year 1976 is equal to *pi*. Entebbe airport with its floor on fire is equal to *pi*.

3.

The opening scene of Spike Lee's *Do the Right Thing* will, if you allow it, have you standing on the sofa's edge for ninety minutes. The dance your heart makes in the closing credits is equal to *pi*. So are the number of times you watch it again as if for the first time.

The world trying to reset itself is equal to *pi*. As is the burden that arouses men to labour. That too is equal to *pi*. Do you notice a pattern? Ok! Don't focus on the spine but on what it holds up. The Future is an eroding witness, and she will tell you that war is not

about protecting the border but about how much blood was spilt within it. Tragedy belongs to such whispers. The bodies of your friends in a morgue are equal to *pi* and whatever flame is burning. Fame in a world like this is worthless – that too equals *pi*.

> *My country is a woman in heat,*
> *a bridge of lusts. Mercenaries cross her,*
> *applauded by the massing sands.* – **Adonis**

IV.

On which Earth am I the conqueror?

CAI

In the summer of 1976, the future dies. Uganda becomes an unfinished sculpture 'paperweighting' a colonial map and even time itself becomes thinner than paper. Give me a wide shot. Wider! See, even the sky is late. In this place – in this kingdom – in this undergrowth, we are the wrong people even to ourselves. Ospreys are in flight in search of a nest. I too am hunting. Away! To the dark that tries to hide us. I am the watchman cloaked in its shadow who left his wife and child asleep in the mud hut. Soon I will become death. I am waiting for a metal bird to land on a runway. Its wings are fanning the air. Here death comes: so be it.

Mecca

Downtown, summer lengthens. Basquiat starts painting
the never-ending night of space with its sonic madness
as if it were water flowing down to the sea. The poet
exits the subway to enter the gallery. In the basement,
he salutes the painter with the words Spirit and Fire.
Which loosely translates to – Forgive this interlude.[1]
I've never been able to find a recording of President[2]
Johnson signing the Treaty on the Non-Proliferation
of Nuclear Weapons. Outside my apartment window,
a patch of grass is trying to become a desert.[3] I bet
a sweat-dripping Johnson, after making love to his
wife in the Oval Office realises that if he lets them push
the button then his grandchildren won't survive. And that's
why he signs. Or is it: Mrs Johnson won't be able to conceive?[4]

Maybe it's when the barber wraps a hot towel around
his face – in that intimacy, the same intimacy men have
when they prepare their parachutes to jump out of a plane,
the same intimacy with which Rameses II's handmaidens wrapped
his body as they hummed his name in a sky devoid of the moon.
Or devoid of his name, that was sugar water in their mouth,
as they massaged the bones of the great hidden God. Maybe,
by the process of elimination, this is how things disappear.
If the ocean disappears will it invite the sun to its house?
If the plane disappears what happens to the hostages?
If Amin disappears who will look after my people. Could
you love my city as if it were your own? Scratch that!

---

1 Scratch that!
2 Scratch that!
                        3 Scratch that!
      4 Scratch that!

in italiano 1983

(The poet asks Basquiat about Sangre as he brushes his teeth)

Let us begin with a crown of thorns.
Why say anything about death its
gravity its grace? My memory has been
gathering thoughts like cargo; my favourites
are the ones in which I have a broken wing
and they mistake me for a bat looking to
the sky beyond. I digress. I dare you to disturb
the universe.

(Meanwhile)

(Distorted sound)
              Become the T V's flicker, a song
as it fades in and out, a commercial break
or that phone blinking on a shelf. There is music
in this. I am wearing a long grey coat against which
I feel the sun sinking, against which the earth
like me is spinning. I took that nameless road
to touch the dust in the world and cast my face
into the silence. The way Camus knew that love
is best with silence. There it is, along the corners,
it splits the city along its seam.

Icarus: a Self Portrait – 1984

I quit my job that Saturday when I heard my name called by the manager.[1] That motherfucker always
looked at me like I was running drugs for some cartel or there was a stain on my pants after coming
from the bathroom. Two months ago,[2] I was drunk[3] in New York with an au pair who was studying to be

a fashion photographer. She was ordering coffee in Harlem when she dropped her change. The barista wrote
her name – Alizée with two e's – on the rim of her latte. That was about the same time the energy embargo
began. Her English was better than my French, but in a fleeting moment of relaxation I offer to pay for her
drink. It was the least I could do. In my mind, I was hearing myself say *let me pay for your hot drink* but what

came out was *Je suis chaud*. And to think I walked in to ask directions. I was already late for my meeting.
As I placed my card on the counter she asked, "What do you mean?"[4] Photographers see the world differently[5]

---

1 I have retreated like this before as though life were
    a vessel chartered for a distant coast.
2 Didn't you notice this new decade lengthening
    as I woke before birds migrating seaward?
3 It is not yet summer, and you know next-to-nothing
    about me, except the old story.
4 I mean, don't leave me to this earth the way
    the wind does, unwinding its portion above us.
5 There is not a combination of sound and shadow
    that I can solidify, that describes my privacies.

from the rest of us.[1] To you and me a day is just a day but to them,[2] it is a gathering
  of time or more

accurately of light. The same light Plato speaks about in the cave. An hour from
  now,[3] we would be sat
by the window[4] talking about migrants cast adrift on flimsy rafts and what Kubrick's
  2001 would have been
like if it had been directed by Orson Welles as her third latte cooled off. Behind me
  white clouds gathered
before the thunderclaps. Alizée was taking pictures while flicking her black hair
  behind her ears. The next

thing I knew, in a moment that I thought was mine, we were in the back of a taxi.[5]
  Someone had left
an issue of *Newsweek* on the seat, opened to page 11. This is where the mythology
  begins. What do you
want to know? That her name means trade wind. Or that a painter can use a myth to
  reinvent what has

happened before. In the same way that we played two jazz cassettes on repeat in her
  hotel room while
making love, only resurfacing for room service and to purchase scalped Dave
  Chappelle tickets at a

---

1 That includes you, reader: there is no word for forget,
        only leaving and even that is a song. Selah!
2 Coming from a point-and-shoot neighbourhood,
        I am looked at from all sides. Ask Caleb.
3 To survive I find ways to make the earth move,
        a persistent rain follows me in the black car.
4 My eyes can't keep pace with the motorbike picking
        up speed. Brake lights have the same motion.
5 The things that abandon you in the front seat.

comedy club in Soho on Friday. I'd be lying if I did not admit we were playing with
  death. Exchanging
what we owned with what we didn't own. It was the nature of recovering what was
  lost until she left for Paris.

A Panel of Experts

Tell me about the first time you met Basquiat. Not this request again . . .
So: Kobe has the ball, Staples Center, they're up by eight against
the 76ers. Two rows behind Jack Nicholson and the lady

he is with, who keeps adjusting her bra. Phil Jackson calls a timeout.
I'm not used to American money, so when the popcorn vendor
offers me my change I say keep it. Some kid asks Basquiat for an autograph.

He's not even paying attention. He's waiting for the timeout to end
so he can watch men stand on the edge of the earth's lip and return
to being birds. There's red paint on his Comme des Garçons suit.

Before combing his Ray-Bans into his dreads he asks me for a pen
like he knows me, still watching the game as if it were a Spanish
tragedy. Time is a real cannibal: the rest of the day plays like the *Zodiac Suite*

on loop. By track five it's Saturday, 3AM. Breakfast is a powerful piece
of technology. So, I order two omelettes and some OJ. We talk for hours
about Joyce – the act of endless beginnings – but the world can't simplify

itself. A TV screen is witnessing a small catastrophe. Basquiat isn't scared
of the hi-tech wolf. So, we climb right into the canvas like a galaxy shivering
and he says *don't be fooled by the never-ending pattern of abstraction. It's the only way*

we can become particles of light. As time becomes a direction he has to leave. I barely
remember, but I think the Lakers won. Of course, the transitions were much
slower. I think he had the remote. Hey! Does that answer your question?

Wasn't it Vallejo who asked, what does the Blackness herald with its hard blows? In a hire car the mountains grow towards us. He says nothing to his agent as she relays instructions down the line. *Make sure you're laughing . . . Talk with your hands, palms facing up – questions like.* The dashboard illuminates as he switches the headlights on. The road ahead starts to reappear along with her voice.

Basquiat talks to the poet about Light

Hollywood Africans

The only thing that was certain was that it was June and we had split a pepperoni pizza between us. An ultraviolet light set off the room. Basquiat channel surfed, looking for cartoons, while Icarus prodded a canvas to see if the image fitted precisely in the frame. He was certain that someone had broken in. I'm getting set to coast towards the front door when the girl of my dreams walks in. Now, I have to make some lame excuse about how I'm off to the bodega to get some smokes and how I have a craving for meat. I am bound by this habit. She just smiles. I smile back. Then a voice from the back of my throat says, *You can come with.* Cut to me and her at a stop sign. I don't want to play the right game the wrong way. In the silence that has followed us from the front door, I swat a crown of mosquitos above her head. There is no water, but I can smell the ocean. The man at the store is sweeping the street – at which point I ask her name. I have only ever seen her in a gallery with a glass of prosecco in her hand. I watch the man watching us, in that night, in that long summer. She pulls out some ice cream from the freezer and adds it to the bill. The pulp of her lips is flint and fire. The birds are silent and so is the wind. The rest of the night falls away. In another magic, she calls me by my original name. It is difficult to know what to walk away from. She asks why my eyebrows are raised. We are sitting on top of a park bench watching time. We are a part of it, right here in New York City. This is where the road delivers us towards the edge of difference. Butterscotch drips from my fingers and falls to the tarmac. A beautiful suspension. Then I or you, or whoever decides to look, hand-rolls a cigarette as we rummage through our back pockets for a light.

The New Carthaginian

In the dark light after the temple incident, after the broken oaths,
after watching my city burn in the night's velvet, everything that

surrounded me emerged as an embrace. First, the wind moaned
and hushed as the trees with slow-growing leaves bent their backs.

Then as the road turned away it occurred to me: why do I not know
what makes this earth a variable star, why do I not know it by

its old name, its gullies and young grasses that break soil, its bushes
and flowers that seek abundances? I am a fallen wire. I am swept dust

that decreases in value. Notice how the river carries the water away?
Notice the hawk's descent and how it aligns with the mountains beyond?

Notice even this envelope of darkness as we are watched by God's eye,
its calligraphy. The distance of its vision is the distance of the sea.

Codex©

CODEX©

Flight is the tendency to move
toward or away from an object.
As in Basquiat's Icarus, for instance.
Notice how everything turns away.
In most versions of my story,
we begin at the airport lounge
in Athens. Each of these men
has a past. The minister
of foreign affairs, the IDF sniper
and the expat are all plausible targets.
All believers in the conscious world
and the world to come but they
have no covenant. (Distorted voice.)
In the spirit of tonight have a listen to this.

CODEX©

SAMO© first appears as a tag on a New York
City wall in 1978 two blocks down from Aswad
bookstore. It is a kind of CODEX© to speak
the unspeakable as if it were a confession on redbrick
or brownstone in the hard years. Downtown
was Jean's street studio. So were the fridge, TV,
wall and floor in the apartment. He saw no division
between earth and sky. To call it graffiti is to call
hieroglyphics gibberish. That's ignorant. This is
Jean-Michel ordering a tequila to test his outer limits.
It's a summer night and we have rented two 35mm
cameras. He's figured out that a painting is stronger
than memory, passports, planes and nicotine.
Curtains drawn. Wood scavenged. Paint and unpaid rent.

After red wine he swears he heard the wall say
– *Let your wrists be free*. In the face of all this,
he was kin to me. This is a photograph of
Jean-Michel after the ten-minute set at the Mudd Club.
He says – *It's not me*, and shows more interest
in the streetlamp above us. Look, the camera is guessing.
Selfhood is a controlled hallucination generated
by the brain. The night is a black moon. The Empire
State building has always been a lead character
in his inner movie. From the loft, it glows orange.
This is Jean-Michel, and he says – *If you can't see
my three-point crown you should see a doctor.*
He is divided and dying for a piss. He presents
as an image of a man and as matter in motion.

CODEX©

In my childhood village, past the dirt road, folding hills
and the fields my father would walk, there are boatmen casting nets
onto the water. These men are possibly the same ones my father knew.
They smoke tobacco and watch the lake with its obsidian glow
as if it were a cure. There is all this water between us. They watch me,
the arrivant, as they throw their weight against a line. They have stirred
the waters. The sun ripples as silver butter catfish swim towards a woman
smoking oil over a charcoal stove. She stokes this small sun as the sun at its
horizon is also watching and fading as the boats come in. The wind is against us.
Flight delayed, watching the metal wing of a plane waiting for us like
a getaway car. The night at the end of the runway trembles. Like the raven,
I wish we could climb up out of these clouds ushered from one life through
to another with only our duffle bags and what they could hold of this city
to where the sky was drifting across the border beyond a mountain's fist.

CODEX©

In this story of falling, a cigarette is brought back to life.
The body inhales. The sky is full of night. Soon it will be
dry season and the hills will rust, but tonight, night keeps
moving the way birds do toward migration. What does
living do for any of us? The winds have found some clouds
to play with as trees rehearse the gesture of surrender.
Do birds think that cities are our version of the open sky?
Have you seen my city on fire? Flames throwing themselves
at buildings the way the sea throws itself on the rocks.
The furnace is the city's costume. This world is a desperate
element. I suffer the shame of asking what happens in the voids.
What shape does the soil take when roots vanish? The visible
making itself known by the invisible. Rain falls through the trees
and the dark brick of our old lives is the pitch of the moment.

CODEX©

Truth be told, as a child I wanted to date Princess (not her real
name) from Battle of the Planets. At the table read of episode 16,
"Rescue of the Astronauts", I figured I'd use my human voice
to unroll the dark and catch an edge of a connection. None of that
corny shit like – *I used to live around here.* I'd start with silence
and when the whites of her eyes caught the whites of my eyes, I would
turn my card and say – *I am the thing that I am.* This loneliness was not
supposed to last forever. If the sky ripened into morning. And if my heart
bounced and kicked when she walked into the room even though we'd
have nothing in common but our laughter (I use mine as a ruse). – The quiver
of a streetlight outside plays a useful distraction. Her hands creep up
my torso towards my sad smile. Although I tack and jibe, the crest
of her palms lodges me in her tenderness. However poorly used, her voice
is a star among the stones. We make a tangled mess in the sheets.

Impatience divines the attraction exerted by the body. I play the blade
and she the sheath. In what exact measure I am uncertain, the tide owns
us now. Halfway through the afternoon, she is laughing a lot.
Certain parts of us that only speak in silence loosen in the swell
of repetitions. A city waits as the night thickens like a flock of birds.
Sometimes, I am the silence that does not mend. Today I am grief-in-waiting,
and this membrane of a smile hides the folds of my life to which no one
returns the same. – Back at the table read, I would pray that my body remain
silent like a body of water, even through her silence, because silence itself
is a kind of flight. And when the director, an anonymous observer, yelled
Cut the way Martin Scorsese would yell *Cut* while filming *Taxi Driver*,
I would observe her kinesis. I'm not saying I'm Robert De Niro.
Look at me: I have my grandparents' face. But what I am saying is that
sometimes the world is a yellow taxi and in those moments, I am

Robert De Niro in a yellow iron box, that yellow coffin floating
around the city. In that kind of reality, the walls won't hold. I know
what you're thinking – *She's not even real*. Neither are these feathers
plucked from Caesar's wing. Three blocks from here there is a billboard
on the side of a factory that offers low price flights to Phuket in a diptych
with an airplane parked on the runway. I know what you're thinking –
Well, what's that got to do with the speed of light. Nothing, if *nothing*
is the code word for *set our people free*. Nothing, if *cartoon* is the code
word for *I can't hurt you*. Take for your consideration Cartoon Law
IX – *Everything falls faster than an anvil*. Or my personal favourite Cartoon
Law III – *Any body passing through solid matter will leave a perforation conforming
to its perimeter*. Also called the silhouette of passage. I am trying to be
both the object falling and the silhouette of passage. The thing is,
in a body like this one, there is always the possibility of side-effects.

CODEX©

Night. A new day crawls forth over dead sparrows. There's no
world, no self. According to the *Times* they want to see a war.
My iPhone develops a sense of its own existence. Pure intelligence.
10:59. Two trucks crossed a border in a country full of summertime.
A dropped word, a soundless approach live from a war, the humming
craft above. After the first shot, the voice wouldn't let go.
The dying, jealous of their own release. No footage or proof. I do
not know who was responsible. As the night broke off into shadows,
what followed was a reconstruction based on available evidence.
The sea collected itself, a public security announcement spoke
from the dark of a pocket radio. Their eyes watched the night
thicken. In the debris of pursuit, mercenaries waited for the sun
to die. Dogs sniffing them out, boots caked in dung. Even light
knows how to panic and finds a way where there is none.

CODEX©

00.21. (START TAPE.) We begin here in
transit; it is September, and I need to invent
a kind of time the way Coltrane did in *Alabama*.
I am looking for a hole in the ground or
lightning from a skinned tree with its fragile
brightness that spikes below the waterline, not
to be seen from the dirt road. Where is my old city
perched on seven hills? Where is the sky in its
height to watch the evening crawl in? Where are
the horses that broke loose? I know I come from
another world that is both sheath and blade, both
bruise and blood. You have me in a room.
Your boss is using my last name outside this door
to express the relationship between me in part

and its whole. The name sounds strange at the edge
of his mouth, like bait at the end of a hook.
I glance at a clock. The ceiling tiles are perforated,
and you ask *Why did I move from the home I once had
to this home?* Your silence is also a hole. The soil
from which I came does not want my return.
In the eighth century men who look like me
came to the hem of your shores. They used
the wind like a stone in a sling. I used an airbridge.
I used a runway. I used a loud flight path. I used
an airport lounge in a country known for its
invading army. I used who I am in this night
with its far-off star. I used what nobody would
admit, that geography is everything. (END TAPE.)

CODEX©

When my father lost his job, it was
a way to make the other thing
a beginning; the sit-ins and marches
with helicopters twitching at 24
frames a second. My father had been
many things, not just a face behind
a thought travelling the free world.
Once he was a glass mountain. Once
he was a catastrophe separating day
from night. Once when we were
at the edge of town and he could
no longer keep the silence he used
the same face he spoke with to cry.
I had a small nonspeaking part.

CODEX©

When death was a winged horse, I escaped
my country by taking a flight south. Clouds
between the sky and us. Between the earth
and us. I devoted my time to the background
turning slowly as engines roared, en route
to a waiting city. The night seemed to comprehend
and answer; it became a guardian that mistook
me for part of itself. Sometimes it was a gate
or face or a document. But as a desert bird
is silent so was I. As the light turned so did
the stretched wings of the plane. Maybe I'm
only here to wait, the way a mountain waits
for the valley below. The way the future waits
for our lives to take place, learning and watching.

CODEX©

Put a man in a room and lock a door.
If he's still alive after you've said a lot
of things, keep him from harm and keep
him in the dark until there is no difference
between this room and the night of space.
As the hours pass he will try to cure
himself of his country. But isn't a country
also a space? The man is now an empty
bottle. I fill it with secrets. These yellow
flowers, which I bought at the service
station, are my daughter's favourite.
That too is a lie. Until you have been
a body collecting flies or a spirit departing
you will never know the world's true form.

CODEX©

Rumi said *Everything that is made beautiful*
and fair and lovely is made for the eye of one who sees.
In 1973, the same year my mother met my father,
Steven Spielberg had just wrapped on *American*
Graffiti. Over black coffees and buttered scones
with George Lucas, Speilberg imagines a movie
about an archaeologist in a leather jacket, a felt
fedora and a three-day beard who carries
a bullwhip and runs around the globe seeking
relics and lost civilisations. Two years later, back
in the US after three weeks of meetings, director
friend Kaufman shares a story that his childhood
dentist (let's call him Michael) would tell him while
he was getting his retainers. (Bite harder.)

Eroica

Eroica 1

I. SAMO© AS AN ALTERNATIVE TO BLAH . . . BLAHBLAHBLAH.
    BLAHZOOEY . . .BBLAHBLAH QUASI-BLAH . . .– – – ETC.

(in Eb major).

Now, I am second guessing, but in principle aren't we worth more
than sparrows? But here too, even after dying and a forced landing
I am lost for words. What can I tell you about the history of violence?
This is our misfortune: to leave hot summers and embrace a forced
migration. The minute I wrote this I became an armed man. If you
ask me, it's time to get out of here. But before we do, what if we go
back and reconnect with our people? Not to the IDF commandos

spraying bullets. They did as ordered. Not to the oligarch with his
overdressed Russian girlfriend or the soldiers asleep in the control
tower awaiting their own destruction. We can skip the passenger
headcount and the follow-up report (salted with fingerprints) by the UN
aviation agency. It tells the story of the diverted passenger flight from
Athens, but excludes the ones boiling beans over a slow fire watching ants
on a chicken bone from the day before. What follows is an account

of the nature of birds or the nature of glory, or the nature of what made
Moses lead us out of Egypt, or the nature of fury. I imagine it's something
you would want to come back to, like this painting that allows us to crash
through the wall of a room. Ever tried it? I know enough about living
to know that the canvas is merely a cluster of spatial theories in the shape
of a landscape. Brake lights. Black car. Notice this new decade lengthening.
It's summer and yet you know next-to-nothing about me, except the old story.

II. SAMO© . . . AS AN END TO BOOSH-WAH . . .

(in C minor)

What follows is a description of an unknown timeline. In December 1969
Thelonious Monk taped a show for French television titled *Jazz Portrait:*
Thelonious Monk. I, Basquiat, would have been nine at the time. This is two years
after Ngũgĩ publishes *A Grain of Wheat.* Flawless! At one point, the text reads,
Then nobody noticed it; but looking back we can see that Waiyaki's blood contained within
it a seed, a grain, which gave birth to a movement whose main strength thereafter sprang from
a bond with the soil. Rewind your mind. Press play. Such erasure should surprise

no one. Anyway, back to Monk. Listening to a live recording is like observing
a low solstice. Deep silence and its imitation meld into a narrative so that you can say,
I was there when. Feel free to add your own peril. Monk's music is devoted
to reversing the silence, in the same way that da Vinci was devoted to discussing
the moon's brightness relative to the sun. Mark their ways and what they capture.
Mark the border, a field's end, that place across the street, the twelve, seagulls
defending the shore, dogs sleeping in mud, airport walls in need of repairs . . . etc.

Mark the harmonic function of everything repeating. A tarmac road leads to
more tarmac roads. With this careful adjustment made, it turns out that if the runway
and plane could speak to each other then we would have a gate in this lengthening
summer. Which is another way of saying June 1976 – red ants have found the trees,
guards are sweating oil. In the background my veins thicken like wings. Sidenote:
my marriage to Madonna would have failed. I treated her face on the *New York Post*
like the Holy City of Safed. At this slip boundary let us use the second act as a getaway
    car.

Eroica 2

III. SAMO© AS AN END TO PLAYING ART

(in E♭ major)

What follows is the same July, its spread of light. In that confusion
picture what it sees and, in that confusion, let us begin. Remember Icarus
is not a name, but an equation of the New Theory of Flight. As I say this I am at
the cliff's edge with my father's voice daring me to jump. The poet will not
paint the city without me. To know what I'm searching for will require calamity,
a nation invading us, a patient day. The West will never share this image.
Assume a painting already knows what it is reaching for as a couple kiss in front

of its frame. The year the Eagles write "Hotel California" the poet's father has formed
a family of his own. At four years old he is already a bastard child. And knows how
to say "You hurt me!" in four languages to the man whose photo never hangs on
the wall because, absent the Eye of God, which sees everything, his life is a mask,
even to members of his own household. Perhaps love scenes are a conversation
(a white background and wooden frame become the border constantly shifting
similar to a point of landing when the coast is constantly shifting), just as a painting

is a conversation. In the fusion of these two events, we now have perfect quorum.
I am many selves. This is our edge. Cut to 47 hostages released for the selfish
ambition of America. Cut to the quiet floor of a runway or the question all bodies
ask, whether living or dead: *Who made me?* Cut to a mangrove fragranced with acorns
near where villagers watch foreign voices growl commands. Notice the flames a bullet
makes when it wants to be heard. Bullet. Bullet. Bullet. There's no suffering after
death, a mind merely swings open. Yo, give me a headcount. In Dilla time.

> Man dies – there are 47 pictures that were never shown.
> Man dies – this plane is nothing but a wooden horse.
> Man dies – but unlike oil on canvas, it is not preserved.

IV. SAMO©/ANOTHER DAY/ANOTHER DIME/HYPER COOL/ ANOTHER WAY 2/KILL SOME TIME

(in E♭ major)

What follows are field notes with some variations on the theme. Fuego! Not all realities
are true. Admit it. What do you know of *saddle point flow?* Rumi said everything that is
    made
beautiful and fair and lovely is made for the eye of one who sees. I'm a man who
    dreams
and this is the dream. How much longer can we afford to wait? In 1976 *Viking* 2 lands
    on Mars.
Its purpose is to make us believe in tomorrow as if it were a number on a dressing
    room mirror.
The mirror is important. Let's assume that Uganda is a story that belongs to the time
    before death
and not a dirty word in the country of our collective future. Death is also a mirror.
    Realising
that this moment of the day goes unnoticed. And that Entebbe is a regular city void of
    winter

scattered with people en masse, fitted with hearts and minds, fitted with concerns of
    the day.
Masking their concerns with smiles. Then how did the Air France plane get here? It is
    a miracle
made possible by the combined effects of (i) incompressibility and (ii) I forget the
    second point.
The Airbus tires on the tarmac voice. Ooh shoo beedee! Faces at a gate become a
    document.
An unnamed person stamps visas for departure. Who fitted the Revolutionary Cell with
    masks?

More importantly, who turned the song of Yoni into an anthem? The first time I heard
     Haitian
Fight Song by Charles Mingus I was in the sky watching the wind prevail, as it pointed
     east so that
it can whisper, *This is what you are.* In the classical Kutta-Zhukovsky circulation theory
     there is no lift

without a sharp trailing edge. Look at the sun burning like ($C_6H_2CH_2$). Like a low
     flame. As I too
float in the space between Entebbe and a star's explosions. Here are a number of
     preoccupations.
What does it mean to be in a room? Even when that room is the night. An Entebbe
     runway is an
ending and part of his beginning, in the same way that DJ Kool Herc invents the Merry-
     Go-Round
and hip-hop begins. Because that is what life is, a turntable to switch between
     breakbeats on two copies
of the same record. True story. Picture this. One thing will become two for anything
     called the way. In the
moon's absence, these equations of inverse proportion are matters taped to the wall of
     my mind.
The most precious things I own. The night grips tight to the evening. How will I let it
     go?

Notes

EXPLODED COLLAGE

In this work, I explore how Basquiat's 'exploded collage' can be used as a poetic device. The exploded collage allows for multiple codices of information and insight to be displayed all at once, free of social hierarchies. To these, Basquiat adds a sampling of experience, the way a DJ samples music. It is an active ingredient that provides paintings, pictures or pages with a new emotional charge. The seemingly nonsensical use of language, symbols, numbers and images are in fact a code for those willing to engage.

I gleaned the phrase 'exploded collage' from the work of one of Basquiat's critics and curators, Diego Cortez. Cortez curated the first public showcase of Basquiat's work, in the MoMA P.S.1 group show 'New York / New Wave' in 1981; he was drawn, he said, to Basquiat's use of line. Later, he became particularly interested in the way Jean-Michel 'explodes' the popular twentieth-century compositional device known as 'collage', which existed from Constructivism and Cubism to Robert Rauschenberg. The exploded collage, Cortez explains, gives physical equality to all particles and was Basquiat's ultimate achievement. In the exploded collage the radical change is in the background, as opposed to the iconic figures Basquiat places in the foreground.

WORKS REFERENCED

Adūnīs, *Adonis Selected Poems* (trans. Khaled Mattawa), Yale University Press, 2010.

Auden, W. H., 'Musée des Beaux Arts' (1938), quoted in *Harper's Magazine*, 30 November 2008.

Bar-Zoha, Michael, *Mossad: The Great Operations of Israel's Secret Service*, Biteback, 2012.

Basquiat, Dir. Julian Schnabel, Hells Kitten Productions, 1996.

The Batman, Dir. Matt Reeves, Warner Bros, 2022.

Becker, Andrew Sprague, *The Shield of Achilles and the Poetics of Ekphrasis*, Rowman & Littlefield, 1995.

Boom for Real, Dir. Sara Driver, 1996, Miramax.

Bruegel, Pieter, *Landscape with the Fall of Icarus*, 1560, Royal Museums of Fine Arts of Belgium, Brussels.

Buchhart, Dieter, Eleanor Nairne and Keith Haring, "Basquiat: Boom for Real." *Remembering Basquiat*. Prestel Publishing, 2017.

Buchhart, Dieter, Mary-Dailey Desmarais, et al., *Music and the Art of Jean-Michel Basquiat*, Editions Gallimard, 2022.

Campt, Tina M., *A Black Gaze: Artists Changing How We See*, MIT Press, 2023.

—— *Listening to Images*, Duke University Press, 2017.

Casali, Sergio, 'Doors of the Temple of Apollo', *The Classical Journal*, 91.1 (1995), pp. 1–9: www.jstor.org/stable/3297769.

Clement, Jennifer, *Widow Basquiat: A Love Story*, Crown Publishing Group, 2014.

Cohen on the Bridge, Dir. Andrew Wainrib, 2009,.

Conrad, Joseph, *Heart of Darkness*, Modernista, 2023.

Dante Alighieri, *Inferno* (trans. Michael Palma), W. W. Norton, 2020.

David, Saul. *Operation Thunderbolt: The Entebbe Raid – the Most Audacious Hostage Rescue Mission in History*. Hachette, 2015.

Dodge, Theodore Ayrault, *Hannibal*, Adamant Media Corporation, 2001.

Dreyfuss, Henry, *Symbol Sourcebook: An Authoritative Guide to International Graphic Symbols*, Wiley, 1972.

Dunstan, Simon, *Israel's Lightning Strike: The Raid on Entebbe 1976*, Bloomsbury, 2012.

Eliot, T. S. *Four Quartets*, Faber & Faber, 2019.

—— *The Waste Land & Other Poems: Including The Love Song of J. Alfred Prufrock*, Penguin, 2019.

Entebbe / 7 Days in Entebbe, Dir. José Padilha, 2018.

Ezrow, Natasha M., and Erica Frantz, *Dictators and Dictatorships: Understanding Authoritarian Regimes and Their Leaders*. A&C Black, 2011.

Garvey, Marcus, ' "Look for me in the whirlwind", Freedom speech', 1924: https://speakola.com/political/marcus-garvey-look-for-me-in-the-whirlwind-1924

Halevi, Aviram, *Entebbe Declassified*, eBook Partnership, 2021.

Hartman, Saidiya V., *Wayward Lives, Beautiful Experiments: Intimate Histories of Social Upheaval*, W. W. Norton, 2019.

Heffernan, James A. W., *Museum of Words: The Poetics of Ekphrasis from Homer to Ashbery*, University of Chicago Press, 2004.

Homer, *The Iliad* (trans. Robert Fitzgerald), Oxford Paperbacks, 2008.

Kotin, Joshua, 'Shields of Construction and Direction: Ekphrasis in the *Iliad* and the *Aeneid*', *Hirundo*, 1 (2001), pp. 11–16.

The Last King of Scotland, Dir. Kevin Macdonald, FilmFour, 2006.

Lowenstam, Steven, 'The Pictures on Juno's Temple in the *Aeneid*', *Classical World*, 87(2) (1993), pp. 37–49.

Mayer, Marc, *Basquiat*, Merrell, 2005.

Netanyahu, Iddo, *Entebbe: A Defining Moment in the War on Terrorism – The Jonathan Netanyahu Story*, New Leaf, 2003.

Ofer, Yehuda. *Operation Thunder: The Entebbe Raid – The Israelis Own Story*, Penguin, 1976.

O'Hara, Frank, *Lunch Poems*, City Lights Publishers, 1964.

Operation Thunderbolt, Dir. Menahem Golan, 1977

Ovid, *Metamorphoses* (trans. David Raeburn), Penguin, 2004.

Peterson, Derek, and Richard Vokes, *The Unseen Archive of Idi Amin*, National Geographic Books, 2021.

Putnam, Michael C. J., 'Dido's Murals and Virgilian Ekphrasis', *Harvard Studies in Classical Philology*, 98 (1998), pp. 243–75.

Quashie, Kevin. *The Sovereignty of Quiet: Beyond Resistance in Black Culture*, Rutgers University Press, 2012.

Raid on Entebbe. Dir. Irvin Kershner, Stockton Metropolitan, 1977.

Ross, Lucinda L., *Gold Griot: Jean-Michel Basquiat Telling (His) Story in Art*, PhD Thesis, University of Plymouth, 2018: http://dx.doi.org/10.24382/1263.

Saggese, Jordana Moore, *Reading Basquiat: Exploring Ambivalence in American Art*, University of California Press, 2021.

—— (ed.) *The Jean-Michel Basquiat Reader: Writings, Interviews, and Critical Responses*, University of California Press, 2021.

Somers, Thierry. 'Jean-Michel Basquiat Collage Constructivism Cubism Archives', *200percent magazine*, 13 October 2017: https://200-percent.com/tag/jean-michel-basquiat-collage-constructivism-cubism/

Stevenson, William. *90 Minutes at Entebbe: The Full Inside Story of the Spectacular Israeli Counterterrorism Strike and the Daring Rescue of 103 Hostages*, Simon and Schuster, 2015.

Stercken, Angela, '[Arte]Fact, Object, Image: Jean-Michel Basquiat's Archives of the Black Atlantic', in Gabriele Genge and Angela Stercken (eds.), *Art History and Fetishism Abroad: Global Shiftings in Media and Methods*, Transcript, 2014, pp. 129–58.

Thompson, Robert Farris, *Aesthetic of the Cool: Afro-Atlantic Art and Music*, Periscope, 2011.

—— *Flash of the Spirit. African and Afro-American Art and Philosophy*, Random House, 1983.

Victory at Entebbe, Dir. Marvin J. Chomsky, Warner Brothers Burbank, 1976.

Virgil, *The Aeneid* (trans. Sarah Ruden), Yale University Press, 2009.

Weizman, Eyal, *Forensic Architecture: Violence at the Threshold of Detectability*, Zone Books, 2017.

Williamson, Tony, *Counterstrike Entebbe*, HarperCollins, 1976.

ACKNOWLEDGEMENTS

Poems from *The New Carthaginians* have appeared in *Across Borders* anthology, *Ambit*, *English: Journal of the English Association*, *Bath Magg*, *Five Dials*, *More Fiya* anthology, *Mapping the Future: The Complete Works Poets*, *The London Magazine*, *Poetry*, *Poesis International*, *Poetry Birmingham Literary Journal*, *Poetry London*, *Poetry Review*, *Poetry Wales*, *Prairie Schooner*, *Rialto*, *The Poetry Archive*, *Wasafiri*, *Wild Court* and *World Literature Today*.

I am eternally grateful to Dr Sarah Howe and Dr Anthony Joseph – for their diligence, support and creative intellect. Thank you to all who critiqued earlier versions of my poems, especially Mimi Khalvati, Professor Ruth Padel, Dr Karen McCarthy Woolf, Roger Robinson, Joe Shakespeare and Dr Denise Saul.

Thank you to the Arts Council England, the Anaphora Writing Residency, The Art Fund, Arvon, The Black Writer's Guild, The British Association for American Studies, The Broad LA, The Brooklyn Museum, Cave Canem, The Community of Writers, Cove Park, Furious Flower, Middlebury Bread Loaf, The Guggenheim Bilbao, The High Museum Atlanta, The Institute of Contemporary Arts, Koko Camden, The London Arts & Humanities Partnership, MACBA Barcelona, The Menil Collection Houston, MOCO Barcelona, The Montreal Museum of Fine Arts, The Museum Boijmans van Beuningen, Rotterdam, The Nahmad Contemporary, The National Gallery, Poet in the City, The Society of Authors, Speaking Volumes, Tate Britain, the Whitney Museum, The MAP Consortium, and The Young Foundation. You individually and collectively gave me a way forward when I thought there was no way. Your 'yes' challenged me and made me into a new creature.

I would personally like to thank the Complete Works programme founded by Bernardine Evaristo, directed by Nathalie Teitler, and funded by the Arts Council. It gave me direction and knowledge about the industry and improved my writing no end.

To the following, for their random acts of kindness: George Szirtes; Momtaza Mehri, Clare Pollard; Eleanor Nairne; Mary-Dailey Desmarais; Nisha Eswaran; Twayna Mayne; Jordana Moore Saggese; Jacob Sam-La Rose; Bernardine Evaristo; Adrian Matejka; Dr Joanne Gabbin; Catherine Barnett; Lauren K. Alleyne; Jennifer Grotz; Lauren Francis-Sharma; Charlie Dark; Nathalie Teitler and the Complete Works family; the Obsidian Foundation family; the Cave Canem family; Lisa Anderson; Tobi Kyeremateng; Nii Ayikwei Parkes; Erica Wagner; Roba Ofili; Maura Dooley; Alby James; Keren Lasme; Jeremy Poynting; Nels Abbey; Fiona Lesley; Dean Ricketts; Kevin Young; Theresa Lola; Marcelle Mateki Akita; Terrance Hayes; Bill Herbert; Kwame Dawes; Aatish Shah; MPK Squad; Jason Allen-Paisant; Benji Reid; Nuar Alsadir, Nicole Sealey; Tishani Dosh; Kate McGrath; Ariana Benson; Peter Kahn: Yomi Sode; Haya Alfarhan, Ella Frears; Joy Francis; Anthony Anaxagorou; Raymond Antrobus; Victoria Adukwei Bulley; Kayo Chingonyi; Caleb Femi, Marion Manning; Rachael Allen; Gregory Pardlo; Margret Busby; Sarala Estruch; Dante Micheaux; Malika Booker; Daniel Maskit; Joseph Kendra; and the late Gboyega Odubanjo.

At David Godwin Associates: thank you, David Godwin, my deepest gratitude for your patience, and your belief in my writing before you even saw one line. Thank you, Aparna Kumar, for always being on 'go', your enthusiasm is electric. I can't wait to see what we will do next.

At Penguin, my publishers, thank you: to the editorial team of Donald Futers, Chloe Currens and Fahad Al-Amoudi for bending time and space to make this happen. You all possess the skill of ruthless honesty and gentle encouragement in equal measure. In this editorial endeavour, you have been true guardians of this work; to the wider Penguin family, you really lived up to that word. Thank you, for holding my heart in your hands without prejudice.

To the late Jean-Michel Basquiat, your paintings, and passion in the work you left behind have been a torch, a key, a mirror and a codex. I also want to thank your sisters Lisane Basquiat and Jeanine Heriveaux for being great custodians of your art and allowing us to get to know the real you in the *King Pleasure* exhibition. This book is also for you and the generosity you show in sharing your brother's legacy with the world.

Finally, there is no way this work would have been completed without the love and grace of God, my wife Johanna, and my two children Iden and Olivia, who are my right and left wings.

EKPHRASTIC IMAGES

Jean-Michel Basquiat, *Pegasus*, 1987.
Jean-Michel Basquiat, *Now is The Time*, 1985.
Jean-Michel Basquiat, *Riddle Me This, Batman*, 1987.
Jean-Michel Basquiat, *Bird of Paradise*, 1983.
Jean-Michel Basquiat, *Untitled (Fallen Angel)*, 1981.
Forensic Architecture, *The Long Duration of a Split Second*, 2019
Jean-Michel Basquiat, *Self-portrait*, 1981.
Jean-Michel Basquiat, *Warrior*, 1982.
Jean-Michel Basquiat, *Cassius Clay*, 1982.
Self-portrait of the poet as 1982.
Jean-Michel Basquiat, *Untitled (Julius Caesar on Gold)*, 1981.
J. M. W. Turner, *The Decline of the Carthaginian Empire*, 1817 (Tate).
J. M. W. Turner, *Dido Building Carthage*, 1815 (National Gallery).
Jean-Michel Basquiat, *Riding With Death*, 1988.
Jean-Michel Basquiat, *Icarus Esso*, 1986.
Jean-Michel Basquiat, *El Gran Espectaculo (The Nile)*, or, *Untitled (History of Black People)*, 1983.
Jean-Michel Basquiat, *Moses and the Egyptians*, 1982.
Jean-Michel Basquiat, *Equals Pi*, 1982.
Jean-Michel Basquiat, *Mecca*, 1982.
Jean-Michel Basquiat, *in Italiano*, 1983.
Jean-Michel Basquiat, *Self-portrait*, 1984.
Jean-Michel Basquiat, *A Panel of Experts*, 1982.
Jean-Michel Basquiat, Hollywood Africans, 1983.
Jean-Michel Basquiat, *Eroica 1 and Eroica 2*, 1988.